Character Values

I Am
a Leader

by Sarah L. Schuette

Consulting Editor: Gail Saunders-Smith, PhD

Consultant: Madonna Murphy, PhD
Professor of Education, University of St. Francis, Joliet, Illinois
Author, *Character Education in America's Blue Ribbon Schools*

Capstone
press®
Mankato, Minnesota

Pebble Books are published by Capstone Press,
P.O. Box 669, 151 Good Counsel Drive, Mankato, Minnesota 56002.
www.capstonepress.com

1 2 3 4 5 6 11 10 09 08 07 06

Library of Congress Cataloging-in-Publication Data
Schuette, Sarah L., 1976–
    I am a leader / by Sarah L. Schuette.
    p. cm.—(Character values)
    Summary: "Simple text and photographs show different ways of being a
leader"—Provided by publisher.
    Includes bibliographical references and index.
    ISBN-13: 978-0-7368-6334-6 (hardcover)
    ISBN-10: 0-7368-6334-6 (hardcover)
    1. Leadership—Juvenile literature. 2. Character—Juvenile literature. I. Title.
II. Series.
BF723.L4S38 2007
158'.4—dc22   2006000516

Note to Parents and Teachers

The Character Values set supports national social studies standards for units on individual development and identity. This book describes leadership and illustrates ways students can be leaders. The photographs support early readers in understanding the text. The repetition of words and phrases helps early readers learn new words. This book also introduces early readers to subject-specific vocabulary words, which are defined in the Glossary. Early readers may need assistance to read some words and to use the Table of Contents, Glossary, Read More, Internet Sites, and Index sections of the book.

Table of Contents

Leadership

I am a leader.

I set a good example for others.

I listen to my dad.
I think carefully
before I make a choice.

8

At Home

I plan a movie night
for my family.
I pick a movie
that everyone likes.

I am a good role model
for my younger sister.
I follow the rules.

At School

I am responsible.
I make sure
my whole group
helps with our project.

14

I am the first one
to volunteer.
I set a good example
for my class.

I am a team captain
in gym class.
I help my team
do its best.

18

I serve others.
I help my friend
with math.

Being A Leader

I am a responsible
and caring leader.
I do what I say
I will do.

Glossary

captain—the leader of a sports team

example—a model for others to follow

responsible—doing what you say you will do; people who are responsible keep promises and follow rules.

role model—someone who others look up to; role models follow rules and make safe choices.

serve—to help someone by giving your time and talents

volunteer—to offer to do something without pay

Read More

Hirschmann, Kris. *Leadership.* Character Education. Chicago: Raintree, 2004.

Parker, David. *I Am a Leader!* The Best Me I Can Be. New York: Scholastic, 2005.

Internet Sites

FactHound offers a safe, fun way to find Internet sites related to this book. All of the sites on FactHound have been researched by our staff.

Here's how:

1. Visit *www.facthound.com*

2. Choose your grade level.

3. Type in this book ID **0736863346** for age-appropriate sites. You may also browse subjects by clicking on letters, or by clicking on pictures and words.

4. Click on the **Fetch It** button.

FactHound will fetch the best sites for you!

Index

Word Count: 120
Early-Intervention Level: 14

Editorial Credits
Amber Bannerman, editor; Jennifer Bergstrom, set designer and illustrator;
    Ted Williams, book designer

Photo Credits
Capstone Press/Karon Dubke, all

The author dedicates this book to her pastor, Robert Broeder of Le Sueur, Minnesota.